A PHOTOGRAPHIC GUIDE TO ARABIC SCRIPT

A PHOTOGRAPHIC GUIDE TO

ARABIC SCRIPT

Andrew Swift

A PHOTOGRAPHIC GUIDE TO
ARABIC SCRIPT

First published 2020
by CheckPoint Press
www.checkpointpress.com

ISBN 978-1-906628-84-0

Contents

Arabic script

- Arabic is written from right to left. This applies to the spelling of the words, to the order of those words in the sentence and to the arrangement of pages in a book. Text flows from the top of the page to the bottom, just as in European languages.
- The Arabic alphabet has 28 fully fledged letters plus a number of semi-official characters formed by the addition of marks above or below (so-called 'diacritics').
- In principle, the characters in Arabic words are joined up just as in handwritten European script. However, there are six letters of the alphabet that will only join with the preceding character, i.e. the one on the right. This leads to internal breaks within words.
- The shape of a letter varies according to its position in the word: initial, medial, final or isolated. Total number of characters to look out for: (22 x 4) + (6 x 2) = 100
- There is no distinction between lower case and upper case (capital) letters.
- Whereas the consonants are always shown, the vowels may be taken for granted. Example: k+t+b (كتب) pronounced 'kitab' = book (singular), but when pronounced 'kutub' = books (plural). Full Arabic orthography has the capacity to display short vowels as diacritic marks above and below other letters, but these are generally omitted – certainly here in the context of public signs.
- Three of the 28 letters perform a dual function, representing either a long vowel or a consonant but never a short vowel: ا = 'a' or glottal stop; و = 'u' or 'w'; ي = 'i' or 'y'.

- The Arabic alphabet is rich in guttural sounds (emanating from the back of the throat) but has only two labial (= lip) sounds, 'b' and 'f'. Consequently, the characters representing these two sounds are also used to indicate the 'p' and 'v' sounds in foreign names.
- Various languages of South-Central Asia, for example Farsi (Iran), Pashto (Afghanistan) and Urdu (Pakistan), use alphabets derived from the Arabic.
- Calligraphy has always been highly esteemed in Arabic culture, not least for religious reasons.

The Arabic alphabet

The Arabic alphabet is displayed on the next four pages in the order traditionally taught to children learning to read their own native language.

The order in which the letters are presented in this book is different, which is why the page numbers are non-sequential.

The way the names of the letters are pronounced varies across the Arabic-speaking world; for example the vowel in ba, ta, tha etc often sounds more like ‘air’ than ‘ah’.

The images have mainly been cropped from photographs that occur later in the book.

Final	Medial	Initial	Isolated	Name/Page
				alif 29
				ba 89
				ta 93
				tha 97
				jim 105
				haa 101
				kha 109
				dal 53

dhal
57
ra
45
zay
49
sin
69
shin
73
Sad
129
Dad
133
Ta
137
DHa
141

ayn
121
ghayn
125
fa
113
qaf
117
kaf
77
lam
35
mim
81
nun
85

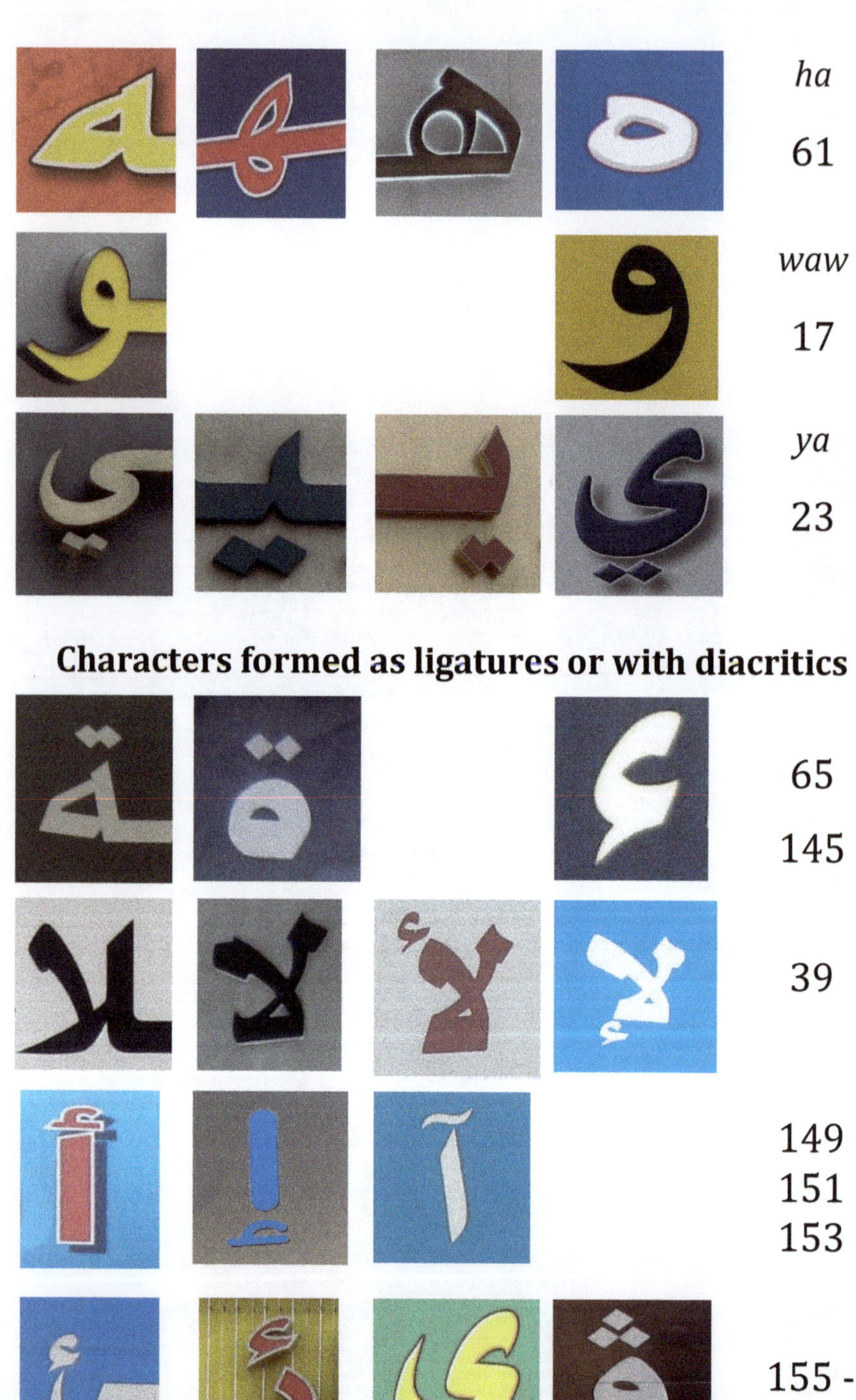

Characters formed as ligatures or with diacritics

Character profiles

The traditional order of letters in the Arabic alphabet is not the most user-friendly sequence for students approaching Arabic from a European perspective. This publication has therefore grouped the characters as follows:

- The three vowel/semi-vowel characters و ي and ا
- The characters ل (easily confused with ا) and لا
- The four non-joining characters ر ز د and ذ
- The character ه and its variant form ة which is not officially a part of the alphabet but is seen frequently at the end of words functioning as a short ‘a’ sound
- The sibilant pair of س and ش
- The easily recognisable pair of ك and م
- The four consonants that resemble a boat with its crew either on board or overboard ن ب ت and ث
- The trio of ح ج and خ
- The number 9 pairing of ف and ق
- The reverse 3 pairing of ع and غ
- The quartet that might seem superfluous to a European ear which is unable to distinguish them from various other letters of the alphabet: ص ض ط and ظ
- Hamza ء which does not quite make it into the official list
- Characters already encountered above but which have undergone a subtle transformation: ڤ أ إ آ ى and ئ
- The numerals 0 to 9 (٠ to ٩)

The IPA symbol quoted in each case shows the pronunciation as represented by the International Phonetic Alphabet.

When pronunciations are given for items of vocabulary that feature in the signs, a bar on top of a vowel (ā, ī or ū) signifies that it is a long vowel.

Final	Medial	Initial	Isolated
ـو	–	–	و

Name of character: waw

Sound approximation: long ‘u’ as in ‘tsunami’; diphthong ‘ou’ as in ‘house’; semi-vowel ‘w’ as in ‘world’

IPA symbol: [uː] or [aw] or [w]

Opportunities:

- Looks like a number 9 or a speech bubble
- 33% chance of it occurring on its own

Risks:

- Final form similar to مـ (initial mim) or ـمـ (medial mim), but waw has a tail that curves round from the right to the left and a larger loop

Ibn Battuta Mall, Dubai

و	ز
u	z

Blue Souq, Sharjah

ن	ـو	ـتـ	لـ	ا	و
n	u	t	l	a	w

Madinat Zayed Shopping Centre, Abu Dhabi

ـو	لـ	ـو	لـ
u	l	u	l

Deira, Dubai

و	ـد	ـنـ	ـو	مـ
u	d	n	u	m

The Dubai Mall

و	ن	و	ف
u	n	u	f

Abu Dhabi

ز	و	ن	ي	م	و	د
z	u	n	i	m	u	d

Abu Dhabi

ر	ا	ك		و	ر	و	يـ
r	a	k		u	r	u	y

Marina Mall, Abu Dhabi

س	تـ	ر	و	ل	و	و
s	t	r	w	l	u	w

Bur Dubai

د	و	ـو	ـيـ	لـ	ـو	بـ
d	u	w	y	l	u	b

Abu Dhabi

ي	لـ	ـو	جـ	ـو	بـ	ـو	لـ
y	l	u	j	u	b	u	l

Final	Medial	Initial	Isolated
ـي	ـيـ	يـ	ي

Name of character: ya

Sound approximation: 'y' as in 'yes'; long 'i' as in 'machine'; halfway between 'i' as in 'bite' and 'a' as in 'late'

IPA symbol: [j] or [iː] or [aj]

Opportunities:

- The only character displaying two dots below the line
- Distinguished by its extravagant low-sweeping tail in the isolated and final forms

Risks:

- Potential for confusion with بـ (initial ba) and ـبـ (medial ba)

Jumeirah Beach Residence, Dubai

ي	و	سـ
y	u	s

Al Fattan Marine Towers, JBR, Dubai

ز	لـ	يـ	د
z	l	i	d

Bur Dubai

ـم	ـيـ	تـ
m	i	t

Ajman

ي	ر	ا	د
y	r	a	d

Madinat Zayed Shopping Centre, Abu Dhabi

ي	ـد	ـيـ	لـ		ب	ـر	ع
y	d	i	l		b	r	‘

Friday Market, Fujairah

ـا	ـيـ	ـر	ـيـ	ـتـ	فـ	ـا	كـ
a	i	r	i	t	f	a	k

Bur Dubai

ي	د	ـا	شـ
i	d	a	sh

Blue Souq, Sharjah

ـد	يـ	ر	ـد	مـ
d	i	r	d	m

Deira, Dubai

ي	ـر	يـ	شـ	بـ
i	r	i	sh	b

Abu Dhabi

ي	ـر	يـ	مـ	أ		ة	د	ا	يـ	عـ
i	r	i	m	a		a	d	a	y	‘

عيادة = ‘īyāda (*clinic*)

ا

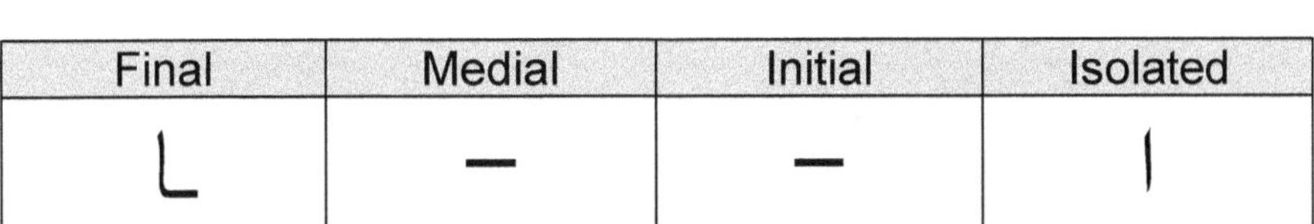

Final	Medial	Initial	Isolated
ـا	—	—	ا

Name of character: alif

Sound approximation: spans the range from long ‘a’ (as in ‘father’) to short ‘e’ (as in ‘Eskimo’); diacritics will also change its sound in some dialects

IPA symbol: [aː]

Opportunities:

- Has a strong vertical presence in the word
- 33% chance of it occurring on its own

Risks:

- When joined to the previous character with a horizontal stroke to the right, it can be confused with لـ (initial lam) or ـلـ (medial lam)

Sheikh Zayed Road, Dubai

ت	ا	ر	ـا	مـ	ا
t	a	r	a	m	a

Deira, Dubai

ـا	ـفـ	لـ	ا
a	f	l	a

Jumeirah Beach Residence, Dubai

ـا	ـبـ	ـمـ	ـا	سـ
a	b	m	a	s

Fotouh Al Khair Centre, Abu Dhabi

و	د	ل	ا
u	d	l	a

Baniyas Square, Deira, Dubai

ر	ا	نـ	ا
r	a	n	a

Abu Dhabi

س	ـا	مـ	ا	د
s	a	m	a	d

Deira, Dubai

ـا	ـيـ	ـلـ	ـا	ـتـ	نـ	ا
a	i	l	a	t	n	a

Abu Dhabi

ج	ـا	تـ	ر
j	a	t	r

Ajman

ق	ـا	فـ	شـ	ا
q	a	f	sh	a

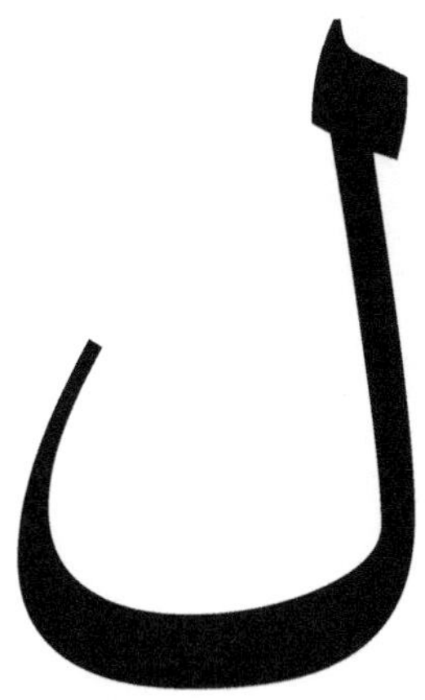

Final	Medial	Initial	Isolated
ـل	ـلـ	لـ	ل

Name of character: lam

Sound approximation: 'l' as in 'lamb'

IPA symbol: [l]

Opportunities:

- Isolated form resembles a capital J

Risks:

- Tail goes in the opposite direction to capital L
- Because of the strong vertical stroke, there is much potential for confusion of the initial and medial forms with alif
- Pronunciation: When followed by certain consonants (the so-called 'sun' group), lam is assimilated to make a double consonant, e.g. al nayzak > annayzak; al turathiya > atturathiya; al rijāl > ar-rijāl al sayidāt >as-sayidāt; al shurta > ash-shurta; al jazīra > ajjazīra

Almaya Supermarket, JBR, Dubai

ل	ـا	ـيـ	ر	ا
l	a	i	r	a

Abu Dhabi

ل	ـا	جـ	ـيـ	ر
l	a	j	i	r

Abu Dhabi

ل	يـ	د	عـ	لـ	ا
l	i	d	‘	l	a

Abu Dhabi

ل	مـ	جـ	أ
l	m	j	a

The Dubai Mall

ل	ـو	مـ		ي	بـ	د
l	u	m		y	b	d

Abu Dhabi

ل	ـا	جـ	ر	لـ	لـ		ـا	ـفـ	لـ	ا		ن	ـو	ـلـ	ـا	صـ
l	a	j	r	l	l		a	f	l	a		n	u	l	a	s

للرجال = lirrijal (*for men*)

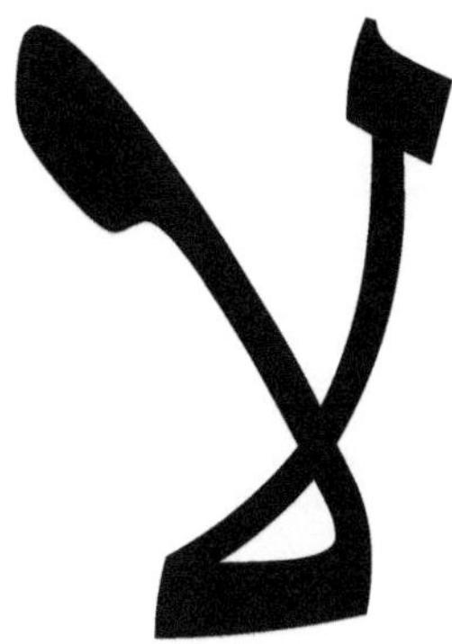

Final	Medial	Initial	Isolated
ﻼ	–	–	ﻻ

Name of character: lam alif

Sound approximation: la

IPA symbol:

Opportunities:

- A so-called 'ligature': lam + alif (Arabic order: ﺎ + ل)
- Avoids confusion of left-facing vertical lam encountering right-facing vertical alif
- Both the isolated form and the final form are unmistakable

Risks:

- Final form looks like it might be spelling alif + lam

Marina Mall, Abu Dhabi

ت	سـ	ـو	كـ	لا
t	s	u	k	la

Abu Dhabi

ـو	لـ	لا		ـة	ـلـ	ـسـ	ـغـ	مـ
u	l	la		a	l	s	gh	m

مغسلة = maghsala (*laundry*)

Heritage Village, Abu Dhabi

ـة	ـلـ	ـا	صـ	لا	ا
a	l	a	s	la	a

Sheikh Zayed Road, Dubai

ـر	ـتـ	لا	فـ		و		ت	ـو	يـ	ز
r	t	la	f		w		t	u	y	z

زيوت و فلاتر = zuyūt (*oil*) wa falātir

Blue Souq, Sharjah

ـا	ـنـ	لا
a	n	la

Corniche, Abu Dhabi

The Dubai Mall

ـك	ـيـ	ـتـ	ـسـ	ـلا	بـ
k	i	t	s	la	b

ت	ـلا	ـيـ	ـز	ـنـ	تـ
t	la	i	z	n	t

تنزيلات = tanzilat (*discount*)

Dubai Autodrome, Motor City, Dubai

ت	ـا	ـمـ	ـلا	ـعـ	ـتـ	سـ	ا
t	a	m	la	‘	t	s	a

استعلامات = īsti‘lamāt (*information*)

Dubai Autodrome, Motor City, Dubai

ة	ـلا	صـ	لـ	ا		ف	ـر	غـ
a	la	s	l	a		f	r	gh

غرف الصلاة = ghuraf (*rooms*) al-salāh (*prayer*)

World Trade Centre, Dubai

ف	يـ	لا
f	i	la

Heritage Village, Abu Dhabi

ـة	مـ	لا	سـ	لـ	ا		ع	مـ
a	m	la	s	l	a		ʿ	m

مع السلامة = ma essalama (*goodbye*)

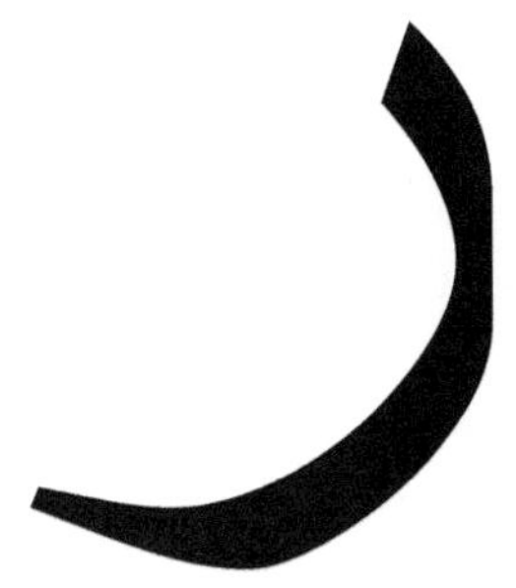

Final	Medial	Initial	Isolated
ـر	–	–	ر

Name of character: ra

Sound approximation: ‘r’ as in ‘red’, but more vigorous, i.e. rolled

IPA symbol: [r]

Opportunities:

- 33% chance of it occurring on its own

Risks:

- Same shape as ز (zay) but minus the dot
- Similar shape to final lam ـل but dips much more below the line

Ibn Battuta Mall, Dubai

و	ر	آ
u	r	’a

Dubai Marina

ا	ر	و	ر	و	أ
a	r	u	r	u	a

Deira, Dubai

ـر	ز	ـيـ	لـ		ـر	بـ	ـو	س
r	z	i	l		r	b	u	s

Abu Dhabi

ـر	ـيـ	ـر	غـ	ـلـ	ا		ـة	ـفـ	ا	ـر	صـ
r	i	r	gh	l	a		a	f	a	r	s

صرافة = sirāfa (*exchange*)

Dubai Marina

ر	ـو	ـفـ	ر	ـا	كـ
r	u	f	r	a	k

World Trade Centre, Dubai

ع	ـيـ	بـ	ـر	ـلـ	ا
‘	i	b	r	l	a

الربيع = al rabī‘ (*springtime*)

Final	Medial	Initial	Isolated
ـز	–	–	ز

Name of character: zay

Sound approximation: 'z' as in 'zero'

IPA symbol: [z]

Opportunities:

- 33% chance of it occurring on its own

Risks:

- Same shape as ر (ra) but with a dot
- Potential for confusion with initial نـ and medial ـنـ (nun)

Abu Dhabi

ز	يـ	لـ	ـا	نـ
z	i	l	a	n

Ajman

ن	يـ	ز	لـ	ا
n	i	z	l	a

Abu Dhabi

و	ز	ر	ـا	مـ
u	z	r	a	m

The Abu Dhabi Mall, Abu Dhabi

ز	يـ	ز	عـ
z	i	z	ʿ

Madinat Zayed Shopping Centre, Abu Dhabi

ز	و	ر	يـ	فـ	لـ	ا
z	u	r	y	f	l	a

Abu Dhabi

ة	نـ	ا	ز	ر	لـ	ا
a	n	a	z	r	l	a

Final	Medial	Initial	Isolated
ـد	–	–	د

Name of character: dal

Sound approximation: ‘d’ as in ‘delta’

IPA symbol: [d]

Opportunities

- Isolated form stands out from the rest of the word
- Isolated form actually bears some resemblance to capital D
- Often found in loan words/names

Risks:

- Final form so upright that it can be confused with medial ـلـ (lam)

Blue Souq, Sharjah

ر	ا	ـد	ـلـ	ا
r	a	d	l	a

Madinat Zayed Shopping Centre, Abu Dhabi

ـا	ـكـ	ـلـ	ـيـ	د		ـز	كـ	ـر	مـ
a	k	l	i	d		z	k	r	m

مركز ديلكا = markaz (*centre*) dilka

Blue Souq, Sharjah

د	ـا	بـ	ـد	ـنـ	سـ
d	a	b	d	n	s

Blue Souq, Sharjah

ـد	ـنـ	و	ـا	ـمـ	د
d	n	w	a	m	d

و	د	ا	ر	و	د	لـ	ا
u	d	a	r	u	d	l	a

Final	Medial	Initial	Isolated
ـذ	–	–	ذ

Name of character: dhal

English approximation: 'th' as in 'these'

IPA symbol: [ð]

Opportunities

- Isolated form stands out from the rest of the word
- Often found in loan words/names

Risks:

- Final form so upright that it can be confused with medial ـنـ (nun)

Sheikh Zayed Road, Dubai

ن	و	ز		ر	ـا	كـ		ا	ذ
n	u	z		r	a	k		a	dh

Abu Dhabi

ـر	يـ	ـذ	نـ		ن	ز	خ	مـ
r	i	dh	n		n	z	kh	m

مخزن نذير = makhzan (*store*) nadhīr

Deira, Dubai

س	و	ـا	هـ		ر	ذ	ـيـ	لـ
s	w	a	h		r	dh	i	l

Al Jafiliya Station, Dubai Metro

ر	كـ	ا	ذ	ـتـ	لـ	ا
r	k	a	dh	t	l	a

التذاكر = atta-dhākir (*tickets*)

Dubai Marina Mall

ر	يـ	كـ	ر	ذ	مـ
r	i	k	r	dh	m

Deira, Dubai

ـل	ـمـ	ـعـ	ـتـ	ـسـ	ـمـ	الـ	ا		ـب	ـهـ	ـذ	ـلـ	لـ
l	m	‘	t	s	m	l	a		b	h	dh	l	l

للذهب المستعمل

= lidh-dhahab (*gold*) almust‘mal (*user*)

Final	Medial	Initial	Isolated
ـه	ـهـ	هـ	ه

Name of character: heh

Sound approximation: ‘h’ as in ‘home’

IPA symbol: [h]

Opportunities:

- Isolated, initial and medial forms are quite distinctive

Risks:

- Four completely different forms
- Final form ـه and isolated form ه are much rarer in practice than the variants with two dots: ـة and ة

Abu Dhabi Fish Market

ه	ـا	ـمـ	يـ
h	a	m	y

يماه = yemāh (*snub nose emperor*)

Mall of the Emirates, Dubai

ـر	ـتـ	ـنـ	سـ		م	ـو	هـ
r	t	n	s		m	u	h

Jumeirah Beach Residence, Dubai

ن	ـو	ـتـ	ـلـ	ـيـ	هـ
n	u	t	l	i	h

Oman

ى	ـهـ	ـقـ	مـ
a	h	q	m

مقهى = maqhā (café)

Abu Dhabi

ـه	ـيـ	ـلـ	ـيـ	فـ
h	i	l	i	f

Blue Souq, Sharjah

ن	فـ	ـو	ـهـ	ـتـ	بـ
n	f	u	h	t	b

Final	Medial	Initial	Isolated
ـة	–	–	ة

Name of character: ta marbutah

Sound approximation: short 'a' as in 'India'; may mask a silent 't' or be followed by a voiced 't'

IPA symbol:

Opportunities:

- Isolated form is unmistakable
- Combination of ه (heh) and ت (ta)

Risks:

- Final form could be mistaken for ق qaf, but ta marbutah leans to the left and the tail goes to the right

Sheikh Zayed Road, Dubai

ـة	ـحـ	ـو	ـد	ـلـ	ا		ـك	ـنـ	بـ
a	h	u	d	l	a		k	n	b

Ajman

ـة	ـيـ	ـسـ	ر	ـد	مـ		ـة	ـلـ	ـفـ	ـا	حـ
a	y	s	r	d	m		a	l	f	a	h

حافلة مدرسية

= hāfila (*bus*) madrasiyya (*school*)

Al Jafiliya Metro Station, Dubai

ة	ـيـ	ـلـ	فـ	ـا	ـجـ	لـ	ا
a	y	l	f	a	j	l	a

Abu Dhabi

ة	ـر	ـيـ	ـسـ	ـمـ	لـ	ا
a	r	i	s	m	l	a

Deira, Dubai

ة	ر	يـ	مـ	لا	ا
a	r	i	m	la	a

الاميرة = al-amīra (*princess*)

Deira, Dubai

ة	ر	جـ	شـ	لـ	ا		ة	كـ	ر	شـ
a	r	j	sh	l	a		a	k	r	sh

شركة = sharika (*company*)

Final	Medial	Initial	Isolated
ـس	ـسـ	سـ	س

Name of character: sin

Sound approximation: ‘s’ as in ‘sierra’

IPA symbol: [s]

Opportunities:

- Distinguished by its extravagant low-sweeping tail in the isolated and final forms

Risks:

- Same shape as ش (shin)
- Medial form ـسـ can get lost in a cluster of ـنـ ـبـ ـتـ and ـيـ

Abu Dhabi

ن	ـا	ـسـ	ـا	سـ
n	a	s	a	s

Madinat Zayed Shopping Centre, Abu Dhabi

ـس	ـيـ	ـو	سـ
s	i	w	s

Deira, Dubai

ـد	ـيـ	ـبـ	سـ		ـر	ـبـ	ـو	سـ
d	i	b	s		r	b	u	s

Fotouh Al Khair Centre, Abu Dhabi

ـر	ـسـ	ـنـ	ـبـ	سـ		و		ـس	ـكـ	ر	ـا	مـ
r	s	n	b	s		wa		s	k	r	a	m

Abu Dhabi

ر	ا	د	يـ	سـ
r	a	d	i	s

Abu Dhabi

ج	نـ	و	سـ	مـ	ـا	سـ
j	n	u	s	m	a	s

Final	Medial	Initial	Isolated
ـش	ـشـ	شـ	ش

Name of character: shin

Sound approximation: 'sh' as in 'short'

IPA symbol: [ʃ]

Opportunities:

- Distinguished by its extravagant low-sweeping tail in the isolated and final forms

Risks:

- Same shape as س (sin)
- Potential for confusion with ـثـ (medial tha)

Ibn Battuta Mall, Dubai

!	ش	ـا	ـمـ	سـ
!	sh	a	m	s

Deira, Dubai

ة	ـر	ـا	ـجـ	ـتـ	ـلـ	لـ		ـا	ـيـ	ـر	ـا	شـ
a	r	a	j	t	l	l		a	i	r	a	sh

للتجارة = littijāra (*trading*)

Abu Dhabi

ي	ـمـ	ـشـ	ـكـ	لـ
i	m	sh	k	l

Mall of the Emirates, Dubai

ن	ـشـ	ـكـ	ـنـ	ـو	كـ		ش	ـنـ	ـر	فـ
n	sh	k	n	u	k		sh	n	r	f

Abu Dhabi

ر	ـو	ـنـ	ـلـ	ا	ـم	شـ
r	u	n	l	a	m	sh

Heritage Village, Abu Dhabi

ـة	ـطـ	ـر	ـشـ	ـلـ	ا
a	t	r	sh	l	a

الشرطة = ash-shurta (*police*)

Final	Medial	Initial	Isolated
ـك	ـكـ	كـ	ك

Name of character: kaf

Sound approximation: 'k' as in 'king'

IPA symbol: [k]

Opportunities

- An interesting character that is instantly recognisable in either of its two very different forms (isolated/final and initial/medial)
- Initial/medial forms resemble an upper case (if rather angular) 'S'

Risks:

- Final and isolated forms have the same shape as ل (lam) with a small floating 's'

Abu Dhabi

ك	ز	يـ	نـ	لـ	ا
k	z	i	n	l	a

النيزك = annayzak (*comet*)

Deira, Dubai

ك	يـ	ر	تـ	ا	بـ
k	i	r	t	a	b

Abu Dhabi

ـش	يـ	نـ	ر	و	كـ	لـ	ا
sh	i	n	r	u	k	l	a

Global Village, Dubai

ك	ـر	كـ		ي	ـا	شـ
k	r	k		y	a	sh

Festival City, Dubai

س	كـ	ر	لا	كـ
s	k	r	la	k

Abu Dhabi

ـب	كـ	ا	ـو	ـكـ	لـ	ا		ـة	ـلـ	ـا	ـقـ	بـ
b	k	a	w	k	l	a		a	l	a	q	b

بقالة = biqāla (*grocery*)

Final	Medial	Initial	Isolated
ـم	ـمـ	مـ	م

Name of character: mim

Sound approximation: ‘m’ as in ‘Miami’

IPA symbol: [m]

Opportunities:

- Distinctive tail on isolated and final form

Risks:

- Possibility of confusion with و (waw) in modern fonts

Dubai Marina

ت	و	يـ	ر	ا	مـ
t	u	i	r	a	m

Abu Dhabi

ى	ـد	ـمـ	ـحـ	مـ		ـم	ـعـ	ـطـ	مـ
a	d	m	h	m		m	‘	t	m

مطعم = mat‘am (*restaurant*)

Dubai Marina

ي	مـ	ـا	ـيـ	مـ
i	m	a	i	m

Abu Dhabi

ـم	ـا	ـمـ	ـتـ	لـ	ا		ن	ـو	لـ	ـا	صـ
m	a	m	t	l	a		n	u	l	a	s

Marina Mall, Abu Dhabi

ل	ـا	ـجـ	ـر	لـ	ا		م	ـا	ـمـ	حـ
l	a	j	r	l	a		m	a	m	h

حمام الرجال = hamām (*bath*) ar-rijāl (*men*)

ـت	ـا	ـد	ـيـ	ـسـ	لـ	ا		م	ـا	ـمـ	حـ
t	a	d	y	s	l	a		m	a	m	h

حمام السيدات = hamām as-sayidāt (*women*)

Final	Medial	Initial	Isolated
ـن	ـنـ	نـ	ن

Name of character: nun

Sound approximation: 'n' as in 'next'

IPA symbol: [n]

Opportunities:

- The boat shape ن is much deeper than ب (ba) and ت (ta)

Risks:

- Initial and medial forms bear a potentially misleading similarity to a handwritten 'i'

Ajman

ن	ـا	ـيـ	ـفـ	سـ
n	a	i	f	s

Gold Souq, Deira, Dubai

ـة	ـيـ	د	ـا	نـ
a	i	d	a	n

Abu Dhabi

ن	ـو	ـنـ	ـا	كـ
n	u	n	a	k

Madinat Zayed Shopping Centre, Abu Dhabi

ـد	ـلـ	ر	و		ن	ـشـ	ـر	ـتـ	ـو	ـيـ	نـ
d	l	r	w		n	sh	r	t	u	y	n

Jumeirah Beach Residence, Dubai

ن	ـا	ـنـ	ـد	عـ
n	a	n	d	ʻ

Friday Market, Fujairah

ن	ـا	ـمـ	ـلـ	سـ		ـة	ـلـ	ـا	ـقـ	بـ
n	a	m	l	s		a	l	a	q	b

بقالة = biqāla (*grocery*)

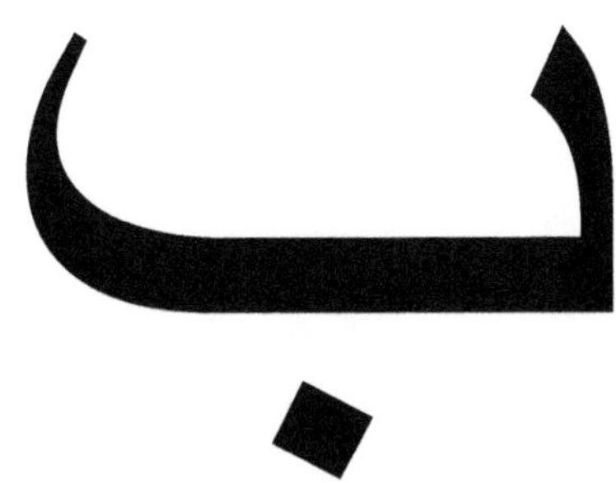

Final	Medial	Initial	Isolated
ـب	ـبـ	بـ	ب

Name of character: ba

Sound approximation: 'b' as in 'best'; also stands in for 'p' in foreign words

IPA symbol: [b]

Opportunities:

- Isolated form resembles boat with man overboard

Risks:

- Medial form does not stand out from the rest of the word in a sequence of ـنـ (nun) ـيـ (ya) ـتـ (ta) ـسـ (sin)
- Initial and medial forms very similar to initial and medial forms of ya: يـ and ـيـ

Blue Souq, Sharjah

ـأ	بـ	سـ
a	b	s

Bur Dubai

ـر	ـبـ	بـ
r	b	b

Ajman

ل	يـ	هـ	و	بـ
l	i	h	u	b

Friday Market, Fujairah

ب	ـا	بـ	شـ	ـلـ	ا		ت	ـلا	يـ	جـ	ـسـ	تـ
b	a	b	sh	l	a		t	la	i	j	s	t

تسجيلات الشباب = tasjilat (*recording*) ash-shabab (*young people*)

Abu Dhabi

ب	و	لـ	نـ	د
b	u	l	n	d

Abu Dhabi

ه	ـا	شـ		ـب	ـيـ	بـ	حـ		ن	ـز	خـ	مـ
h	a	sh		b	i	b	h		n	z	kh	m

مخزن = makhzan (*store*)

Final	Medial	Initial	Isolated
ـت	ـتـ	تـ	ت

Name of character: ta

Sound approximation: 't' as in 'tin'

IPA symbol: [t]

Opportunities:

- Isolated form resembles boat with crew of two

Risks:

- Medial form fails to stand out when flanked by ـنـ (nun) ـيـ (ya) ـبـ (ba) or ـسـ (sin). Initial and medial forms very similar to initial and medial forms of nun: نـ and ـنـ

The Abu Dhabi Mall, Abu Dhabi

ت	س	ک	ن
t	s	k	n

Blue Souq, Sharjah

و	ت	ن	ا	م
u	t	n	a	m

Dubai Marina

ل	ا	تـ	و	تـ
l	a	t	u	t

Madinat Zayed Shopping Centre, Abu Dhabi

ت	يـ	و	كـ	لـ	ا		ر	جـ	تـ	مـ
t	i	w	k	l	a		r	j	t	m

متجر = matjar (*shop*)

Deira, Dubai

ج	ـا	تـ	لـ	ا
j	a	t	l	a

Abu Dhabi

ـي	بـ	نـ	تـ	مـ	لـ	ا		ـة	بـ	تـ	كـ	مـ
i	b	n	t	m	l	a		a	b	t	k	m

مكتبة = maktaba (*bookshop/library*)

Final	Medial	Initial	Isolated
ـث	ـثـ	ثـ	ث

Name of character: tha

English approximation: ‘th’ as in ‘think’

IPA symbol: [θ]

Opportunities

- Distinctive three dots
- Found mainly in loan words/names

Risks:

- Potential for confusion with ت or شـ

ي	ـتـ	ـفـ	ـيـ	ـر	ثـ
y	t	f	i	r	th

Abu Dhabi

ب	ـقـ	ـا	ـثـ	لـ	ا
b	q	a	th	l	a

Abu Dhabi

ن	ـا	ـمـ	ـثـ	عـ		ـو	بـ	أ		ن	ـو	ـلـ	ـا	صـ
n	a	m	th	‘		u	b	a		n	u	l	a	s

Abu Dhabi

ـة	يـ	ر	قـ	لـ	ا
a	i	r	q	l	a

القرية = alqarya (*village*)

ـة	يـ	ثـ	ا	ر	تـ	لـ	ا
a	i	th	a	r	t	l	a

التراثية = atturathiya (*heritage*)

Final	Medial	Initial	Isolated
ـح	ـحـ	حـ	ح

Name of character: ha

Sound approximation: a more heavily aspirated 'h' than ه (heh)

IPA symbol: [ħ]

Opportunities

- Isolated and final forms recognisable by sickle shape below the line
- Base shape for a group of three: ح (ha) ج (jim) خ (kha)

Risks:

- Initial and medial forms not very distinct from final ـد (dal)

Sheikh Zayed Road, Dubai

ح	لا	صـ
h	la	s

Friday Market, Fujairah

ح	لا	فـ		و	بـ	ا
h	la	f		u	b	a

World Trade Centre, Dubai

م	تـ	ـا	حـ
m	t	a	h

Global Village, Dubai

س	ا	ـر	فـ		ت	ـا	ـيـ	ـو	ـلـ	حـ
s	a	r	f		t	a	y	w	l	h

حلويات = hulwiyyat (*sweets*)

Abu Dhabi

ـن	ـيـ	ـمـ	ـر	حـ	لـ	ا
n	i	m	r	h	l	a

Abu Dhabi

ـي	ـبـ	ظ		ـو	بـ	أ		ـح	ـر	ـسـ	مـ
i	b	dh		u	b	a		h	r	s	m

مسرح أبو ظبي = masrah (*theatre*) abū dhabī

Final	Medial	Initial	Isolated
ـج	ـجـ	جـ	ج

Name of character: jim

Sound approximation: sound represented by 's' in 'leisure'; also 'j' as in 'jam'; in Egypt, hard 'g' as in 'go', hence used to show that sound in foreign words and names

IPA symbol: [ʒ] or [dʒ]

Opportunities

- Isolated and final forms recognisable by sickle shape below the line
- Member of a group of three: ح (ha) ج (jim) خ (kha)

Risks:

- Position of dot vital in distinguishing between ج (jim) and خ (kha)

Abu Dhabi

ب	ج	ر
b	j	r

Madinat Zayed Shopping Centre, Abu Dhabi

ة	ر	يـ	ز	جـ	لـ	ا
a	r	i	z	j	l	a

الجزيرة = ajjazīra (*the island*)

Abu Dhabi

ل	ا	ـر	نـ	جـ
l	a	r	n	j

Abu Dhabi

ـا	يـ	ا	ـد	ـهـ	لـ	ا		ج	ـر	بـ
a	y	a	d	h	l	a		j	r	b

برج الهدايا = burj (*tower*) al-hadāyā (*gifts*)

Ajman

ج	و	ر	ع	لـ	ا
j	u	r	ʻ	l	a

Abu Dhabi

ج	ر	خ	مـ
j	r	kh	m

مخرج = makhraj (*exit*)

Final	Medial	Initial	Isolated
ـخ	ـخـ	خـ	خ

Name of character: kha

Sound approximation: the ‘ch’ consonant in Scottish ‘loch’; a throaty fricative sound

IPA symbol: [x]

Opportunities

- Isolated and final forms can be recognised by sickle shape below the line
- Member of a group of three: ح (ha) ج (jim) خ (kha)

Risks:

- Initial and medial forms not very distinct from final ـذ (dhal)

Abu Dhabi

ـن	ـشـ	ـا	ـخـ	مـ		ن	بـ		ـد	ـيـ	ـعـ	سـ
n	sh	a	kh	m		n	b		d	i	‘	s

Ajman

ـز	ـيـ	ـر	ـطـ	ـتـ	ـلـ	لـ	ـخ	ـيـ	ـر	ـمـ	ـلـ	ا
z	i	r	t	t	l	l	kh	i	r	m	l	a

للتطريز = littatrīz (*embroidery*)

Bur Dubai

ـا	ـنـ	ا	ر	ـو	خـ
a	n	a	r	u	kh

Abu Dhabi

ل	ـو	خـ	ـد	لـ	ا		ع	ـو	ـنـ	ـمـ	مـ
l	u	kh	d	l	a		‘	u	n	m	m

ممنوع الدخول

= mamnū‘ (*forbidden*) ad-dakhūl (*entry*)

Géant Hypermarket, Ibn Battuta Mall, Dubai

ة	يـ	تـ	ا	ذ	لـ	ا		ة	مـ	د	خ	لـ	ا
a	y	t	a	dh	l	a		a	m	d	kh	l	a

الخدمة الذاتية

= al-khidma (*service*) adh-dhātiya (*self*)

Jumeirah Beach Residence, Dubai

ـد	يـ	ا	ز		خ	يـ	شـ	لـ	ا		ق	يـ	ر	ط
d	y	a	z		kh	i	sh	l	a		q	i	r	ta

Final	Medial	Initial	Isolated
ـف	ـفـ	فـ	ف

Name of character: fa

Sound approximation: ‘f’ as in ‘first’

IPA symbol: [f]

Opportunities:

Risks:

- Possibility of confusion with ق (qaf), but the tail of ف is flatter
- Possibility of confusion with medial ـغـ (ghayn), but the oval loop of ـفـ is tall whereas the oval loop of ـغـ is flat

Abu Dhabi

ف	ـا	فـ
f	a	f

Blue Souq, Sharjah

ـل	ـيـ	ـر	فـ
l	i	r	f

Baniyas Square, Deira, Dubai

ـي	ـفـ	ـطـ	لـ
i	f	t	l

Global Village, Dubai

م	ـا	ـشـ	لـ	ا		ـل	ـفـ	ـلا	فـ
m	a	sh	l	a		l	f	la	f

Abu Dhabi

ـة	يـ	ـا	فـ	كـ	لـ	ا
a	y	a	f	k	l	a

Blue Souq, Sharjah

ف	ر	ـا	ـعـ	ـمـ	لـ	ا
f	r	a	ʻ	m	l	a

Final	Medial	Initial	Isolated
ـق	ـقـ	قـ	ق

Name of character: qaf

Sound approximation: similar to ‘k’ but much further back in the throat; no vibration

IPA symbol: [q]

Opportunities:

- Looks a bit like a ‘q’, apart from the horizontal tail and two dots

Risks:

- Possibility of confusion with ف (fa); shape slightly different
- Possibility of confusion with medial ـغـ and final ـة
- Tail can be flat or curved; loop can be high or low

Abu Dhabi

ف	قـ
f	q

قف = qif (*stop*)

Oman

ـم	كـ		٢	٠	٠		ط	قـ	سـ	مـ
m	k		2	0	0		t	q	s	m

Jumeirah Emirates Towers, Dubai

ف	قـ	ا	ـو	مـ
f	q	a	w	m

مواقف = mawāqif (*parking*)

Abu Dhabi

د	ـو	ـمـ	ـحـ	مـ		ق	ر	ـا	ط
d	u	m	h	m		q	r	a	t

Abu Dhabi

ـة	لـ	ـا	قـ	بـ
a	l	a	q	b

بقالة = biqāla (*grocery*)

ـر	ـمـ	قـ	لـ	ا
r	m	q	l	a

القمر = alqamar (*moon*)

ق	ر	ز	لا	ا
q	r	z	la	a

الازرق = al'azraq (*blue*)

Final	Medial	Initial	Isolated
ـع	ـعـ	عـ	ع

Name of character: ain

Sound approximation: a weak ‘r’ further back in the mouth, not as strong as a full glottal stop

IPA symbol: [ʕ]

Opportunities:

Risks:

- A challenging character that has four completely different forms
- Identical to غ (ghayn) minus the superscript dot
- Medial form ـعـ could be confused with medial ـمـ (mim)
- Represented in Roman script by a left-handed inverted comma, i.e. a figure 6 ‘. (Figure 9 ’ is used to show hamza glottal stop.)

Deira, Dubai

د	يـ	ا	ز		ع	د	بـ
d	y	a	z		ʻ	d	b

Bur Dubai

ق	و	سـ	لـ	ا		ع	ر	ـا	شـ
q	u	s	l	a		ʻ	r	a	sh

Abu Dhabi

ـت	ـا	ـفـ	ـر	عـ		ـة	ـيـ	ـلـ	ـد	ـيـ	صـ
t	a	f	r	‘		a	y	l	d	y	s

صيدلية عرفات = saydaliyat ‘arafat

Abu Dhabi

ـع	ـيـ	ـا	شـ
‘	y	a	sh

Abu Dhabi

ف	ـا	ـعـ	ـسـ	إ
f	a	‘	s	i

إسعاف = is‘af

Abu Dhabi

ـد	ـيـ	ـمـ	ـعـ	لـ	ا
d	i	m	‘	l	a

Final	Medial	Initial	Isolated
ـغ	ـغـ	غـ	غ

Name of character: ghayn

Sound approximation: similar to initial sound in French 'rouge'; strong vibration, often compared to gargling sound

IPA symbol: [ʁ] OR [ɣ]

Opportunities:

Risks:

- A challenging character that has four completely different forms
- Identical to ع (ayn) apart from the superscript dot
- Medial form ـغـ easily confused with medial ـفـ (fa)

Muscat, Oman

غ	ـا	تـ		د	ر
gh	a	t		d	r

Abu Dhabi

ي	ز	ـا	غـ
i	z	a	gh

Bur Dubai

و	بـ	يـ	ر	غ
u	b	i	r	gh

Blue Souq, Sharjah

ر	ـا	غ	د	لـ	ا
r	a	gh	d	l	a

Abu Dhabi

ي	ـبـ	ظ	ـو	ـبـ	ا		ـة	ـلـ	ـسـ	ـغـ	مـ
i	b	dh	u	b	a		a	l	s	gh	m

مغسلة = maghsala (*laundry*)

Abu Dhabi

ـر	ـيـ	ـد	ـغـ	الـ	ا		ن	ـو	ـلـ	ـا	صـ
r	i	d	gh	l	a		n	u	l	a	s

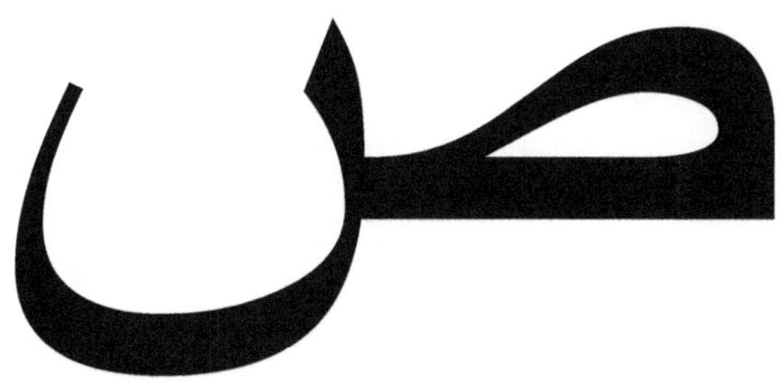

Final	Medial	Initial	Isolated
ـص	ـصـ	صـ	ص

Name of character: Sad

Sound approximation: 's' as in 'sardine' (tongue curled back)

IPA symbol: [$s^{ʕ}$]

Opportunities:

Risks:

- Same basic shape as ض (Dad) but minus the superscript dot
- Learners of Arabic have difficulty distinguishing the sound of this character from س (sin)

Gold Souq, Deira, Dubai

ف	ص	لا	ا
f	s	la	a

Abu Dhabi

ص	ـا	قـ	و		ـو	بـ	ا		ـز	ـبـ	ـخـ	مـ
s	a	q	w		u	b	a		z	b	kh	m

مخبز = makhbaz (*bakery*)

Deira, Dubai

د	ـا	يـ	صـ	لـ	ا
d	a	y	s	l	a

Abu Dhabi

ـن	ـيـ	ـحـ	ـلـ	ـا	ـصـ	ـلـ	ا		ر	ـا	د		ـة	ـبـ	ـتـ	ـكـ	مـ
n	i	h	l	a	s	l	a		r	a	d		a	b	t	k	m

مكتبة = maktaba (*bookshop/library*)

Dubai Creek

ت	لا	ـا	صـ	تـ	ا
t	la	a	s	t	a

(ETISALAT: Telecommunication services and technology company headquartered in UAE)

Final	Medial	Initial	Isolated
ـض	ـضـ	ضـ	ض

Name of character: Dad

Sound approximation: 'd' as in 'dark' (tongue curled back)

IPA symbol: [dˤ]

Opportunities:

Risks:

- Same basic shape as ص (Sad)
- Superscript dot makes it look similar to ظ (DHa)
- Learners of Arabic have difficulty distinguishing the sound of this character from د (dal), ذ (dhal) and/or ظ (DHa)

Madinat Zayed Shopping Centre, Abu Dhabi

ـض	ـا	ـيـ	ـر	لـ	ا
d	a	y	r	l	a

Bur Dubai

ـة	ـيـ	ضـ	ا	ر
a	i	d	a	r

Abu Dhabi

ن	ـا	ـمـ	ضـ
n	a	m	d

Ajman

ن	ـا	ـضـ	ـيـ	ـفـ	ـلـ	ا
n	a	d	y	f	l	a

الفيضان = al fayadān (*flood*)

Abu Dhabi

ر	ـفـ	ـسـ	ـلـ	لـ		ـة	ـضـ	ـيـ	ـو	ـعـ	لـ	ا
r	f	s	l	l		a	d	i	w	‘	l	a

للسفر = lil safar (*travel*)

Bur Dubai

ض	ـيـ	بـ	لا	ا	ؤ	ـلـ	ؤ	ـلـ	لـ	ا
d	y	b	la	a	u	l	u	l	l	a

Final	Medial	Initial	Isolated
ـط	ـطـ	طـ	ط

Name of character: Ta

Sound approximation: 't' as in 'tarnish' (tongue curled back)

IPA symbol: [tˤ]

Opportunities:

- A character that does not change its shape
- Stands out clearly above the line, looking like 'b'

Risks:

- Same basic shape as ظ but minus the superscript dot
- Learners of Arabic have difficulty distinguishing the sound of this character from ت (ta)

Abu Dhabi

س	ـلـ	ط	ا
s	l	t	a

Abu Dhabi

ق	ـفـ	ـشـ	لـ	ا		ـط	ـو	ـيـ	خـ
q	f	sh	l	a		t	u	y	kh

Muscat, Oman

ـم	ـعـ	ـطـ	مـ
m	‘	t	m

مطعم = mat‘am (*restaurant*)

Sheikh Zayed Road, Dubai

ت	ا	ر	ـا	ـطـ	إ
t	a	r	a	t	ay

إطارات = itārāt (*tyres*)

Friday Market, Fujairah

ـب	يـ	ط	لـ	ا	ـت	ـكـ	ر	ـا	ـمـ	ـر	ـبـ	ـو	سـ
b	y	t	l	a	t	k	r	a	m	r	b	u	s

Abu Dhabi Fish Market

ط	ـا	ـبـ	خـ
t	a	b	kh

خباط = khabāt (*Indo-Pacific king mackerel*)

Final	Medial	Initial	Isolated
ـظ	ـظـ	ظـ	ظ

Name of character: DHa

Sound approximation: either ‘th’ as in ‘these’ or ‘z’ as in ‘zero’ (or somewhere in between)

IPA symbol: [ðˤ] or [zˤ]

Opportunities:

- A character that does not change its shape
- Stands out clearly above the line, looking like ‘b’ with a dot

Risks:

- Same basic shape as ط
- Learners of Arabic have difficulty distinguishing the sound of this character from ذ (dhal) and/or ز (zay)

Abu Dhabi

ـر	فـ	ظـ
r	f	dh

Dubai Marina

ي	بـ	ظ		ـو	بـ	أ		ي	بـ	د
i	b	dh		u	b	a		y	b	d

Abu Dhabi

ـت	ـنـ	ـر	ـتـ	ـنـ	ـلا	لـ		ـر	ـظـ	ـنـ	ـمـ	لـ	ا
t	n	r	t	n	la	l		r	dh	n	m	l	a

Khalidiya Mall, Abu Dhabi

ـم	ـيـ	ـتـ	يـ		ـت	ـا	ر	ـا	ظـ	نـ
m	i	t	y		t	a	r	a	dh	n

نظارات = nadh-dhārāt (*glasses*)

Dubai Marina

ـر	ظـ	تـ	نـ	إ
r	dh	t	n	ay

إنتظر = īntadhir (*wait*)

Final	Medial	Initial	Isolated
ء	—	—	ء

Name of character: hamza

Sound approximation: glottal stop used to cut off final vowel

IPA symbol: [ʔ]

Opportunities:

- Appears only at the end of a word in its isolated form

Risks:

- Looks like initial عـ (ayn)
- Also used as a diacritic, e.g. أ
- Represented in Roman script by a right-handed inverted comma, i.e. a figure 9 ’. (Figure 6 ‘ is used to show ayn.)

Abu Dhabi

ء	ـا	ضـ	فـ	لـ	ا
’	a	d	f	l	a

Abu Dhabi

ء	ـا	ـمـ	سـ	أ		ـة	ـلـ	ـا	قـ	بـ
’	a	m	s	a		a	l	a	q	b

بقالة = biqāla (*grocery*)

Ajman

ء	ـا	فـ	و	لـ	ا
’	a	f	w	l	a

Abu Dhabi

ء	ـا	قـ	ـد	ـصـ	لا	ا		ـت	ا	ر	ـا	ظـ	نـ
’	a	q	d	s	la	a		t	a	r	a	dh	n

الاصدقاء = al asdiqā’ (*friends*)

Eppco Service Station, Ajman

ء	ـا	مـ		ء	ا	ـو	هـ
'	a	m		'	a	w	h

ماء = mā' (*water*)   هواء = hawa'

Final	Medial	Initial	Isolated
ـأ	–	–	أ

Name of character: alif with hamza above

Sound approximation: pronounced ‘a’ with preceding glottal or serves to show that a following و is a full vowel (oo) rather than a semi-vowel (w).

IPA symbol: [a] or [ʕ]

Opportunities:

- 33% chance of it occurring on its own

Risks:

- Similar to alif with hamza below إ

Abu Dhabi

ـر	ـيـ	ـبـ	مـ	أ		ـا	يـ	ـر	ـيـ	ـتـ	فـ	ـا	كـ
r	i	b	m	e		a	i	r	i	t	f	a	k

Waitrose Supermarket, Dubai Marina

ـو	مـ	و	أ
u	m	u	'

Final	Medial	Initial	Isolated
ـإ	–	–	إ

Name of character: alif with hamza below

Sound approximation: short ‘i’ as in ‘indigo’ or ‘e’ as in ‘Emirates’

IPA symbol:

Opportunities:

- 33% chance of it occurring on its own

Risks:

- Similar to alif with hamza above أ

Abu Dhabi

ت	ا	ر	ـا	مـ	لإ	ا
t	a	r	a	m	le	a

Jumeirah Lakes Towers Metro Station, Dubai

ت	ا	ر	ـا	ط	ـقـ	ـلـ	ا		ـى	ـلـ	إ
t	a	r	a	t	q	l	a		a	l	i

إلى القطارات = ila al qitārāt

Final	Medial	Initial	Isolated
ـآ	–	–	آ

Name of character: alif madda

Sound approximation: a glottal alif followed by long alif

IPA symbol:

Opportunities:

- 33% chance of it occurring on its own

Risks:

- Similar to alif with hamza above أ

Abu Dhabi

ـا	ـيـ	ر	آ		ـك	ـيـ	ـتـ	ـو	بـ
a	i	r	’ā		k	i	t	u	b

Adnoc Service Station, Al Ain

ـي	ـلـ	آ		ـل	ـيـ	ـسـ	غـ
i	l	’ā		l	i	s	gh

غسيل آلي = ghasīl (*wash*) ’āli (*machine*)

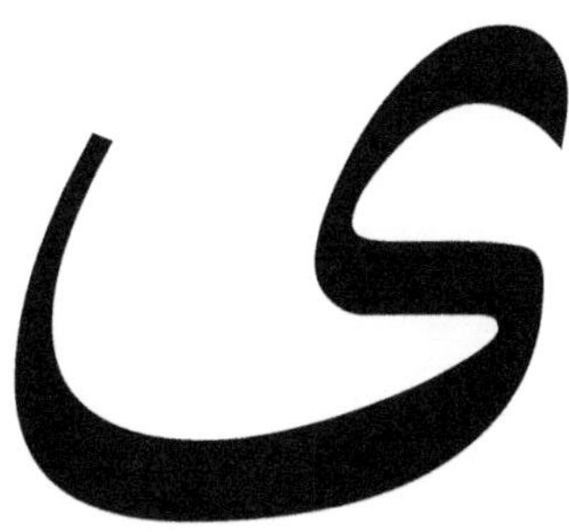

Final	Medial	Initial	Isolated
ى	–	–	ى

Name of character: alif maqsura

Sound approximation: found only at the end of few words; usually pronounced as a long ‘a’

IPA symbol:

Opportunities:

- Distinguished by its extravagant low-sweeping tail in the isolated and final forms

Risks:

- Potential for confusion with ya ي and ya with hamza ئ

Dubai Marina

ي	بـ	د		ى	سـ	ر	مـ
y	b	d		a	s	r	m

مرسى = marsā (*marina*)

Abu Dhabi

ء	ـا	يـ	ز	لأ	لـ		ى	ر	ـا	ـفـ	سـ
’	a	y	z	la	l		a	r	a	f	s

للأزياء = lil aziya’ (*fashion*)

Final	Medial	Initial	Isolated
ـئ	ـئـ	ئـ	ئ

Name of character: Ya with hamza

Sound approximation: various vowel sounds

IPA symbol:

Opportunities:

- Distinguished by its extravagant low-sweeping tail in the isolated and final forms

Risks:

- Potential for confusion with ya ي and alif maqsura ى

Jumeirah Road, Dubai

ئ	ر	ا	و	ط	لـ	ا
y	r	a	u	t	l	a

الطوارئ = al-tawari'

Deira, Dubai

ل	ئـ	ـا	بـ	قـ	لـ	ا
l	y	a	b	q	l	a

Final	Medial	Initial	Isolated
ڤ	ـڤـ	ڤـ	ڤ

Name of character: veh

Sound approximation: 'v' as in 'very'; used only for foreign words and names

IPA symbol: [v]

Opportunities:

- Derived from fa ف by applying a triple array of dots
- Its presence is always a clue that the entire word has been transcribed from another language

Risks:

Jumeirah Beach Residence, Dubai

ك	يـ	بـ	نـ	ڤـ	و	مـ
k	i	b	n	v	u	m

Abu Dhabi

س	و	ـا	هـ		ـر	ـنـ	ڤـ	و	ـر	جـ
s	w	a	h		r	n	v	u	r	j

Numbers

The term 'Arabic numerals' is ambiguous in English, because it can refer either to the numbering system that was introduced to Europe from North Africa in the 10th century (New Arabic numerals) replacing/supplementing Roman numerals or to Old Arabic numerals that are still used alongside the new system throughout the Arabic-speaking world.

Roman numerals

I	II	III	IV	V	VI	VII	VIII	IX	X

NB: There is no symbol representing zero

New 'Arabic numerals' (i.e. Western)

1	2	3	4	5	6	7	8	9	10

Old Arabic numerals (i.e. as used by speakers of Arabic)

١	٢	٣	٤	٥	٦	٧	٨	٩	١٠

Old Arabic numerals operate in the same direction as Western numerals, with the higher unit on the left and the lower unit on the right, e.g. 1928 = ١٩٢٨

one

١

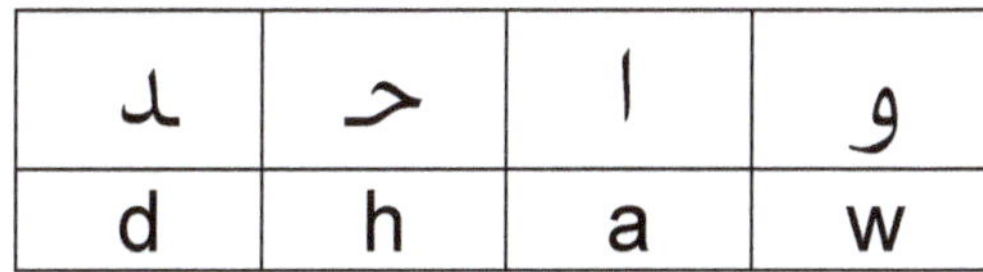

د	ح	ا	و
d	h	a	w

واحد

wāhid

Jumeirah Road, Dubai

١		م	ق	ر		ة	ب	ا	و	ب
1		m	q	r		a	b	a	w	b

bawwāba (*gate*) raqam (*number*) wāhid (*one*)

two

ن	ـا	ـنـ	ثـ	إ
n	a	n	th	i

إثنان

ithnān

Festival City, Dubai

Oman

three

ة	ثـ	لا	ثـ
a	th	la	th

ثلاثة

thalātha

Abu Dhabi

ة	فـ	يـ	ـلـ	خـ		ع	ر	ـا	شـ
a	f	i	l	kh		‘	r	a	sh

شارع = shāri‘ (*street*)

four

ة	ـعـ	بـ	ر	أ
a	ʿ	b	r	a

أربعة

arbʿa

Jumeirah Beach Residence, Dubai

ـة	ـع	ـا	سـ		٢	٤
a	ʿ	a	s		2	4

ساعة = sāʿa (*hour*)

five

ـة	ـسـ	ـمـ	خـ
a	s	m	kh

خمسة

khamsa

Géant Hypermarket, Ibn Battuta Mall, Dubai

ص	ـا	خـ		ـر	ـعـ	سـ
s	a	kh		r	‘	s

سعر خاص = si‘r (*price*) khas (*special*)

٦

six

ـة	ـتـ	سـ
a	t	s

ستة

sitta

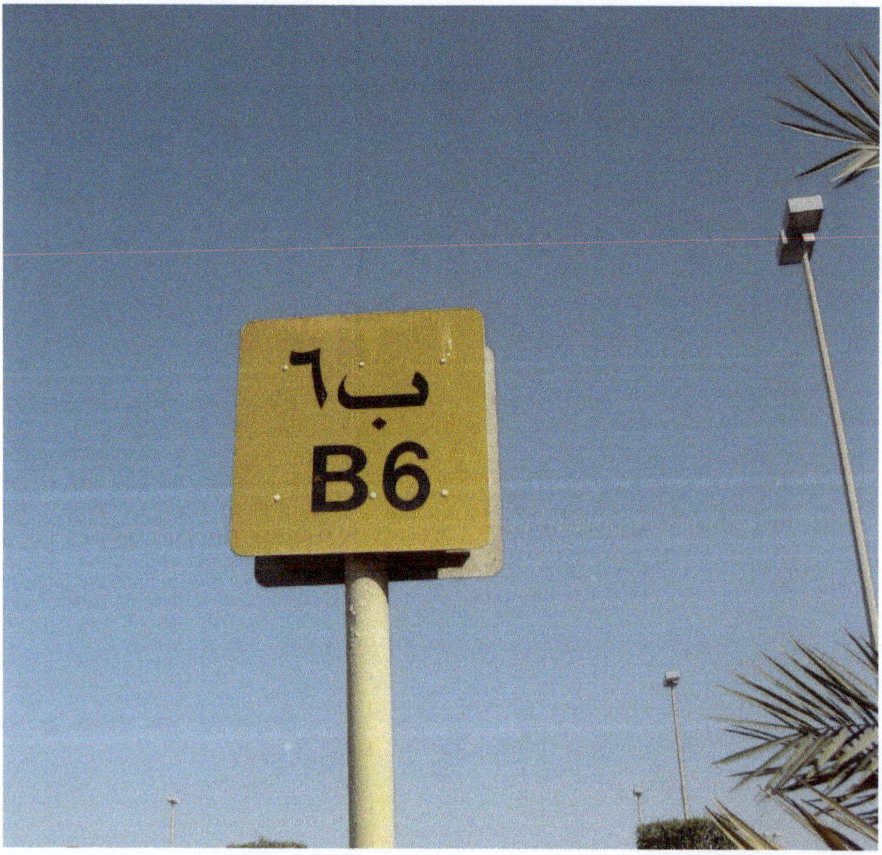

Marina Mall, Abu Dhabi

seven

ـة	ـعـ	ـبـ	سـ
a	‘	b	s

سبعة

sab‘a

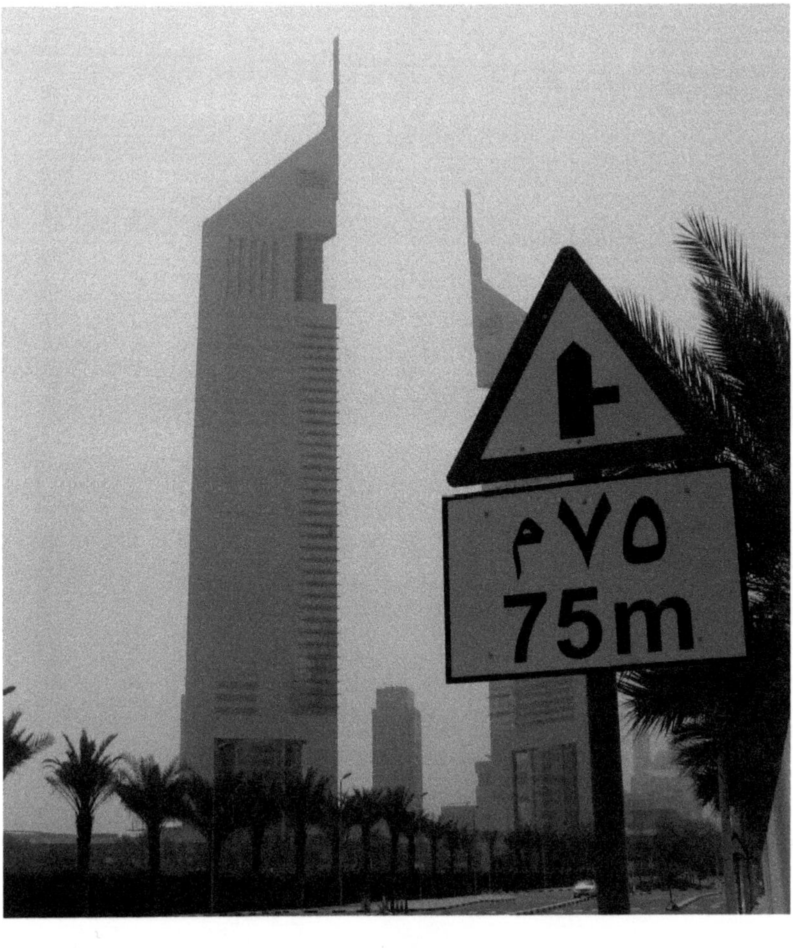

Jumeirah Emirates Towers, Dubai

eight

ـة	ـيـ	ـنـ	ـا	ـمـ	ثـ
a	y	n	a	m	th

ثمانية

thamāniya

Marina Mall, Abu Dhabi

٩

nine

ـة	ـعـ	ـسـ	تـ
a	‘	s	t

تسعة

tis‘a

Abu Dhabi

zero

ر	ف	ص
r	f	s

٠ صفر

sifr

م	ه	ر	د		١	٠
m	h	r	d		1	0

عشرة درهم = a‘shara (*ten*) dirham

Reading practice

Reading practice

Solutions on pages 178 - 180

01

02

03

04

05

06

07

08

09

10

11

12

13

14

دبنهامز
وي كير
صيدلية
شو مارت
بترهومز
ألفا داتا
امريكان بد
بوردرز
يلوهات
بريجستون
ماجيستيك
بالاس
مطعم
فودسيتي
الاسكا

29
بريستول
ميدل ايست باكت سليوشن
30
باور ماجيك
نيوتريشن
31
لابريوش
32
سنتر بوينت
33
بيج أند فت
للأغذية والملابس الرياضية
34
فورتي وان
لتأجير السيارات
35
بوكبلوس
36
ليدر سبورت
37
هومز 4 يو
38
توني روماس
39
كوينز جارد
40
ميك أب
فور ايفر

Reading practice

Solutions from pages 175 - 177

01

02

03

04

05

06

07

08

09

10

11

12

13

14

15

17

16

18

19

20

21

22

23

24

25

26

27

28

29

30

31

32

33

34

35

36

37

38

39

40

Fun with fonts

Sign writers in the UAE take the same degree of professional pride in their work as anywhere in Europe or America. An additional challenge that they face is recreating the style of the corporate font used by multinational retailers.

Abu Dhabi

classical

Abu Dhabi

traditional

Abu Dhabi

modern

Abu Dhabi

bold

Abu Dhabi

austere

Abu Dhabi

minimalist

Dubai Marina

sans serif

Abu Dhabi

with serif

Abu Dhabi

exaggerated serif

Abu Dhabi

diwani

Abu Dhabi

techno

Abu Dhabi

mogul

Festival City, Dubai

corporate 1

Madinat Zayed Shopping Centre, Abu Dhabi

corporate 2

Abu Dhabi

corporate 3

Dubai Marina

party style

Abu Dhabi

superstar

Abu Dhabi

frayed ends

About the author

Andrew Swift is a former teacher of modern languages at a secondary school near Nottingham. He is now a freelance translator. The idea for *A Photographic Guide to Arabic Script* came to him on an extended visit to the United Arab Emirates when he realised that the bilingual shop names and street signs were an ideal visual aid for teaching the rudiments of the Arabic alphabet to beginners in the language. He toured the main streets, souqs and malls of Dubai, Abu Dhabi, Sharjah, Ajman and Fujairah taking more than 4,000 photos which he then sorted into a reader-friendly order.

Acknowledgements

I am especially grateful to **Dr Otared Haidar** of the Department of the Islamic World and Middle East Studies at the University of Oxford for checking and correcting the spellings and transliterations of the Arabic content as well as for her helpful suggestions with regard to the comments sections of this book.

Permission was sought from and given by local proprietors at the time when their premises were photographed.

In the case of international trademark owners, all reasonable steps were taken to seek permission. We received no refusals to our requests, and some rights holders were kind enough to write back giving their express approval. We are therefore especially grateful to the following:

- Domino's Pizza
- Mothercare plc
- Hilton Worldwide Holdings Inc
- Marks & Spencer Group plc
- C. & J. Clark International Ltd
- Unilever
- Mövenpick Hotels & Resorts

www.ingramcontent.com/pod-product-compliance
Lightning Source LLC
Chambersburg PA
CBHW041718090426
42739CB00018B/3466

9781906628840